CATS

MANX CATS

STUART A. KALLEN

ABDO & Daughters

Published by Abdo & Daughters, 4940 Viking Drive, Suite 622, Edina, Minnesota 55435.

Library bound edition distributed by Rockbottom Books, Pentagon Tower, P.O. Box 36036, Minneapolis, Minnesota 55435.

Printed in the United States.

Cover Photo credit: Peter Arnold, Inc.
Interior Photo credits: Peter Arnold, Inc. pages 9, 13, 15, 17, 21

Animals, Animals, pages 11, 19

Edited by Rosemary Wallner

Library of Congress Cataloging-in-Publication Data

Kallen, Stuart A., 1955   Manx cat / Stuart A. Kallen.
    p.   cm. — (Cats)
Includes bibliographical references (p. 24) and index.
Summary: Presents information about the cat which comes from the Isle of Man and is the only cat in the world without a tail.
  ISBN 1-56239-449-5
l. Manx cat—Juvenile literature. [1. Manx cat. 2. Cats.] I. Title. II. Series: Kallen, Stuart A., 1955- Cats.
SF449.M36K35   1995
636.8'23—dc20   95-12655
                                                                              CIP
                                                                              AC

ABOUT THE AUTHOR
Stuart Kallen has written over 80 children's books, including many environmental science books.

Contents

LIONS, TIGERS, AND CATS

THE MIDDLE EAST

Turkey

Lebanon
Israel
Syria
Iraq
Iran
(Persia)

Egypt
Jordan
Kuwait
Qatar
Saudi
Arabia
United Arab
Emirates

Oman

Yemen

Few animals are as beautiful and graceful as cats. And all cats are related. From the wild lions of Africa to the common house cat, all belong to the family **Felidae**. Wild cats are found almost everywhere. They include cheetahs, jaguars, lynx, ocelots, and **domestic** cats.

People first **domesticated** cats around 5,000 years ago in the Middle East. Although humans have tamed them, house cats still think and act like their bigger cousins.

All cats—from cheetahs to the domestic house cat—are related.

MANX CATS

Manx cats come from the Isle of Man, an island off the west coast of Great Britain.

Some types of Manx cats have no tail! For some reason, the cats' tails do not grow.

Many **myths** and **legends** try to explain why these cats have no tails. Some say the cats lost their tails during the Great Flood that is written about in the Bible. The myth says that Manx cats caught their tails in a door when they were late getting onto Noah's Ark.

However it happened, the Manx is the only **breed** in the world that has cats without tails. Today, **breeders** on the Isle of Man have set up a **cattery** to breed the pure Manx cat.

Manx cats come from the Isle of Man, an island off the west coast of Great Britain.

IRELAND

Isle of Man

GREAT BRITAIN

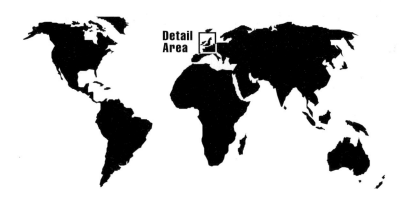

Detail Area

WHAT THEY'RE LIKE

Manx cats are active, friendly, clever, and trusting. They love to play games. Their owners can train them to fetch like a dog.

Some Manx cats have more of a tail than others. Manx cats with no tail are called "rumpies." Manx cats with a tiny tail are called "risers." Manx cats with an even longer tail are called "stumpies." And Manx cats with the longest tails are called "longies."

Manx cats with no tail are called "rumpies."

COAT AND COLOR

Manx cats are shorthaired animals. Their coats may be colored like other cats. They come in white, black and white, red tabby, gray tabby, or **tortoise-shell**.

Manx cats are shorthaired animals. Their coats may be colored like other cats.

SIZE

The playful manx has a small body with a round head, broad chest, arched back, and high rump. The rear legs are heavily muscled and longer than the front legs. The cat runs with a rabbit-like hop.

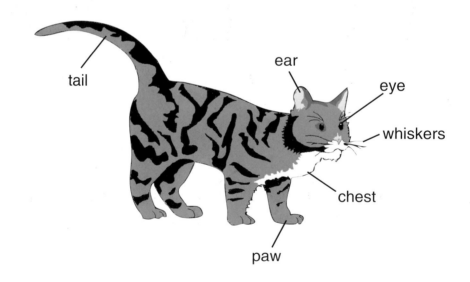

tail

ear

eye

whiskers

chest

paw

Most cats share the same features. But some types of Manx cats do not have tails.

Because of their long hind legs, Manx cats have an unusual hopping walk.

CARE

Manx cats are strong and independent. But like all cats, they love a good brushing. Besides making the cat purr, brushing a Manx cat will keep its loose hair off the furniture. **Grooming** a Manx cat will also keep **hair balls** from forming.

Like any pet, Manx cats need a lot of love and attention. Cats make fine pets. But Manx cats still have some of their wild **instincts**. Cats are natural hunters and do well exploring outdoors.

A scratching post where the cat can sharpen its claws saves furniture from damage. Cats bury their waste and should be trained to use a litter box. Clean the box every day.

Manx cats love to play. A ball, **catnip**, or a loose string will keep a kitten busy for hours.

Manx cats still have wild instincts and are natural hunters that like to explore the outdoors.

FEEDING

Cats eat meat and fish. Hard bones that do not splinter help keep their teeth and mouth clean. Water should always be available. Most cats survive fine on dried cat food. Kittens drink their mother's milk. However, milk can cause illness in adult cats.

Manx cats like to drink milk. However, milk can cause illness in adult cats.

KITTENS

Female cats are **pregnant** for about 65 days. They give birth from two to eight kittens at a time. The average cat has four kittens. Kittens are blind and helpless for the first several weeks.

After about three weeks, they will start crawling and playing. At this time they may be given cat food. After about a month, kittens will run, wrestle, and play games.

If the cat is a **pedigree**, it should be registered and given papers at this time. At 10 weeks, the kittens are old enough to be sold or given away.

Kittens are blind and helpless for the first several weeks. After about three weeks, they will start crawling and playing.

BUYING A KITTEN

The best place to get a Manx cat is from a **breeder**. Cat shows are also good places to find kittens.

Next, you must decide if you want a pet or a show winner. A basic Manx can cost about $50, with blue-ribbon winners costing as much as $500. When you buy a Manx, you should get **pedigree** papers that register the animal with the Cat Fanciers Association.

When buying a kitten, check it closely for signs of good health. The ears, nose, mouth, and fur should be clean. Eyes should be bright and clear. The cat should be alert and interested in its surroundings. A healthy kitten will move around with its head held high.

The Manx cat.

GLOSSARY

BREED - To raise or grow; also, a kind or type.

BREEDER - A person who breeds animals or plants.

CATNIP - A strong-smelling plant used as stuffing for cat toys.

CATTERY - A place that breeds and cares for cats.

DOMESTICATE (doe-MESS-tih-kate) - To tame or adapt to home life.

FELIDAE (FEE-lih-day) - The Latin name given to the cat family.

GROOMING - Cleaning.

HAIR BALLS - Balls of fur that gather in a cat's stomach after grooming itself by licking.

INSTINCT - A way of acting that is born in an animal, not learned.

LEGEND - A story handed down from generation to generation.

MYTH - A story that attempts to explain something in nature.

NON-PEDIGREE - An animal without a record of its ancestors.

PEDIGREE - A record of an animal's ancestors.

PREGNANT - With one or more babies growing inside the body.

TORTOISE-SHELL (TOR-tuss-shell) - A cat that is black, cream, and red in color.

Index

BIBLIOGRAPHY

Alderton, David. *Cats*. New York: Dorling Kindersley, 1992.

Clutton-Brock, Juliet. *Cat*. New York: Alfred A. Knopf, 1991.

DePrisco, Andrew. *The Mini-Atlas of Cats*. Neptune City, N.J.: T.F.H. Publications, 1991.

Swantek, Marjan. *The Manx Cat*. Neptune City, N.J.: T.F.H. Publications, 1987.

Taylor, David. *The Ultimate Cat Book*. New York: Simon & Schuster, 1989.